She Tries Her Tongue,
Her Silence Softly Breaks

WESLEYAN POETRY

She Tries Her Tongue,
Her Silence Softly Breaks

M. NourbeSe Philip

WITH A FOREWORD BY
EVIE SHOCKLEY

WESLEYAN UNIVERSITY PRESS
MIDDLETOWN, CONNECTICUT

Wesleyan University Press
Middletown CT 06459
www.wesleyan.edu/wespress
Manufactured in the United States of America
Typeset in Calluna and Calluna Sans
by Passumpsic Publishing
First Wesleyan University Press edition 2015
Originally published in Canada in 1989 by Ragweed Press

Library of Congress Cataloging-in-Publication Data
Philip, Marlene Nourbese, 1947–
[Poems. Selections]
She tries her tongue, her silence softly breaks /
M. NourbeSe Philip; with a foreword by Evie Shockley.
     pages ; cm
ISBN 978-0-8195-7567-8 (softcover : acid-free paper)—
ISBN 978-0-8195-7568-5 (ebook)
1. Title.
PR9199.3.P456A6   2015
811'.54—dc232015002746

5 4 3 2

For all the mothers

Contents

Her Tongue Tries She

(or How NourbeSe Philip Breaks English
 to Fit Her Mouth)

Luck can play a great role—shockingly so—in bringing someone to the poetry she wants, or even needs, to read.

Someone, reading this volume, is having a very lucky day. Perhaps this person first encountered M. NourbeSe Philip's poetry in the powerful book *Zong!*, floundered in those quietly troubled waters for a time, in over her head, slowly learning that she was not entirely lost, that she could swim with Philip's words, that she could breathe in the space between them—that, in some sense, this poetry was her natural habitat.

Perhaps this person is new to Philip's work, as yet unaware of how the poet can take a word and hold it up to the light to see what it obscures, what it refracts, what it illuminates; can blow air into it to hear its song, its call, its howl; can crack it open; can use it to open us.

Perhaps this person knows her luck, is a long-standing member of that unmarked body of Philip devotees, initially formed circa 1989, composed of those who, once dispossessed of their languages, have regained their voices under her poetic tutelage, who identify one another through the ritual exchange of alchemical (pass)words? *She Tries Her Tongue* (this reader whispers urgently, and I fervently reply), *Her Silence Softly Breaks*...

I was introduced to Philip's writing almost twenty years ago, in a course called New World African Literature (taught by the irrepressible black Canadian poet and scholar, George Elliott Clarke). In the context of James Baldwin's eloquent social analysis, Dionne Brand's politicized lyricism, Dany Laferrière's playful provocations, and Ntozake Shange's defiantly vernacular self-determination, Philip's prize-winning collection of poetry was both right at home and utterly unique. I remember being mystified, yet strangely compelled by the unpredictable ways the pages of her book offered up language. I was lucky to have such a sure and daring guide as Philip be the first to lead me off the charted paths.

The collection includes an essential essay: part autobiography, part Caribbean cultural criticism, part literary theory, and part critical race studies. In it, Philip carefully gives her readers a crash course in what they need to know—about the Caribbean values (at least among people of African descent in Tobago and Trinidad) that shaped her youth, about Caribbean immigrants in Canada, about postcoloniality (as the status of the Caribbean *and* of Canada), and about the transatlantic slave trade, as all these subjects relate to her need, desire, and ability to use language for self-expression, to write poetry. I had some of the necessary knowledge. Having grown up as one of Shange's "colored girls"—"outside" Nashville, "outside" Chicago, and, at that point in my life, "outside" Durham, NC—I understood how speech tasted that came from what Philip calls "the linguistic rape and subsequent forced marriage between African and English tongues." I'd been having the same dish that Philip's poems serve up, just with different seasonings. Shange's characters' search for self in cities across the United States ("bein alive & bein a woman & bein colored is a metaphysical dilemma / i havent conquered yet") was akin to the desperate search of Philip's Caribbean Ceres for her stolen daughter Proserpine:

> is pinch somebody pinch and tell me,
> up where north marry cold I could find she—
> Stateside, England, Canada—somewhere about,
>
> . . .
>
> ". . . stop looking for don't see and can't—
> you bind she up tight tight with hope,
> she own and yours knot up in together;
> although she tight with nowhere and gone
> she going find you, if you keep looking." ("Clues")

Philip, born and raised in Tobago and Trinidad, and living as an adult through Toronto's winters, might be read as metaphorically staging the Caribbean woman immigrant's bifurcated identity through this mother-daughter relationship: bonds stretched, but not broken. The immediate facts and representation of the split were different, but in whatever location, we were women "double-imaged / doubly imagined / dubbed dumb," as Philip writes in "Eucharistic Contradictions," "with a speech spliced and spiced / into a variety of life and lies."

Philip's Caribbean and Canadian experiences are not mine, but they will be intimately familiar to some readers. Maybe one such reader is the "Girl with the flying cheek-bones" or the "woman with a nose broad / As her strength"; maybe another is "the man with the full-moon lips / Carrying the midnight of colour." Of these African Caribbean readers (and of all "New World Africans" whose roots are in exile), her poetry asks:

If not in yours
      In whose
In whose language
      Am I
If not in yours
      Beautiful ("Meditations on the Declension of Beauty . . .")

It is up to these readers to name her features—our features—with words that carry a positive charge, to make the English words express the loveliness and desirability of her body—our bodies—in the face of centuries of connotations to the contrary.

To her African Caribbean readers, in particular, she asserts in her essay (and I, reading along over here, overhear): "For too long, . . . we have been verbal or linguistic squatters, possessing adversely what is truly ours." (Yes, Philip's legal training manifests itself in this volume as in *Zong!* and elsewhere.) Not only is this fabulously musical, rhythmic, elastic "Caribbean demotic" your language, she argues—that which Kamau Brathwaite earlier in the same decade had called "nation language," and which poets like "Miss Lou" Bennett (earlier) and Linton Kwesi Johnson (contemporarily) have shown to be so versatile, so ingenious, and so penetrating, as well. But *also*, Philip insists, the "Queen's English" is yours by right, no matter how hostile it has been to your (our) humanity, no matter how difficult the expression of an African(-descended) self may be in that language. (African Americans have similarly inherited both the heroic couplets of Phillis Wheatley and the best of the Black Arts Movement's black aesthetics. We might cite Tracie Morris's twenty-first-century soundscape "From Slave Sho' to Video aka Black but Beautiful" as work whose telling permutations ring in tune with Philip's "Meditations": "ain't she beautiful," "she ain't beautiful," "boot-boot booty-full," "she too beautiful," "she too black"). This is not a project of "transcending" (as some would put it) the linguistic baggage English carries, of putting it all behind us, so to speak. Rather, Philip sees the "challenge . . . facing the African Caribbean writer" as that of "us[ing] the language in such a way that the historical realities"—the role of English in brutalizing and dehumanizing African people—"are not erased or obliterated, so that English is revealed as the tainted tongue it truly is."

Her poems meet this challenge head-on in a number of ways, some of which will appeal especially to readers who, like me, bring to this book an investment in "postmodern" or "innovative" aesthetics. Some of the strategies that have led to Philip's frequent association with both language poetry and conceptual poetry are employed in her arresting poem "Discourse on the Logic of Language." Though it is technically four pages, I read it as two two-page spreads, each of which contains four "voices" speaking in distinct discourses. One speaks in a recognizably "poetic" discourse; this text, which is lineated and centered on the left-hand page, progresses via repetition, with subtle but powerful variations. Another, represented in italics and located in the right margin of the left-hand page, announces "edicts" in a legal discourse. A third, in the left margin of the left-hand page, in all capital letters and landscape orientation, offers a storytelling discourse. And the last "voice" dominates the whole right-hand page; like the first, it is in normal typeface, but its unlineated paragraphs communicate through the "objective" discourse of education: the prose of a textbook or reference volume. To speak of these discourses as "voices" reminds us that we "hear" or associate different tones with the kinds of language used in the different contexts (the commanding tone of the lawgiver, the matter-of-fact authority of the educator, and so forth). This terminology also highlights the role of the visual in the production of speech effects in written poetry—the poem's *polyvocality* is expressed through very *writerly* devices. A discourse (in the sense of a formal, lengthy discussion of a subject) can be either written or spoken, and Philip's poem harnesses both these possibilities together.

The poem analyzes and unpacks the questions concerning language that her essay addresses: the poem a piercingly beautiful and achingly brutal collage; the essay, precise prose of stunning insight. As theoretical treatments of the same issues in two different genres—and discourses—the two works reenact the formal structure of the poem within the larger framework of the book. (Indeed, the essay functions as both echo and elaboration for virtually all the poems in the collection.) The opening stanza brilliantly crystallizes the "dilemma" that the African Caribbean writer, in Philip's account, always faces:

English
is my mother tongue.
A mother tongue is not
a foreign lan lan lang
language
l/anguish
  anguish
—a foreign anguish.

The other discourses of the poem comment more or less obliquely on this central problem. The legal discourse demands that "slaves" be prevented (by separation) from speaking in the languages they were born to in Africa, lest they "foment rebellion." The narrative discourse tells a story of childbirth and of the "mother's tongue" licking her daughter clean. The final discourse educates us about the brain, parts of which—parts that are critical to our capacity for speech—are named for doctors who worked hard to make science of their prejudices, to demonstrate that white men's brains made them "superior to women, Blacks, and other peoples of colour." English is a tongue that dirties some of us, and the pain it can cause is in no way foreign to our experience of it. Yet it is the tongue with which we must expose and negotiate this very problem.

The final poem in the collection is the title poem, "She Tries Her Tongue; Her Silence Softly Breaks"—at sixteen pages, the longest poem in the book and one in which Philip marshals all the knowledges and all the strategies she has developed up to that point. The poem opens with a simple yet elegant lyricism that joins syntactic patterns derived from the Caribbean demotic (patterns which have become her rhetorical signature) with allusions to Greek mythology, in a stanza whose fourteen gorgeous (unrhymed, unmetered) lines gesture toward the English literary tradition's beloved sonnet form. Her theme is mourning, an elegy for the catalogue of losses brought on by the transatlantic slave trade, cemented in the middle passage, and renewed in every generation:

> the me and mine of parents
> the we and us of brother and sister
> the tribe of belongings small and separate,
> when gone. . .
> on these exact places of exacted grief
> i placed mint-fresh grief coins
> sealed the eyes with certain and final;
> in such an equation of loss tears became
> a quantity of minus.
> with the fate of a slingshot stone
> loosed from the catapult pronged double with history
> and time on a trajectory of hurl and fling
> to a state active with without and unknown
> i came upon a future biblical with anticipation

Losses this vast necessarily result in change, transformation, metamorphosis, and thus possibility. Into this space cleared by tragedy rush a slew of discourses, among them: advice ("The Practical Guide to Gardening"), instruction ("How to Build Your House Safe and Right"), inventory ("oath moan mutter chant"), and prayer ("foreign father forgive / . . . / this lack of tongue"). The poem speaks with the voices of anger, irony, wisdom, and desire. In elliptical, fragmented, cerebral, and deeply felt lines and sentences, it tells how one might survive the loss of almost anything . . . almost everything.

Someone wants—someone needs—this poetry. Luckily, it is here for us again, in a beautiful new edition. Whether we come to be healed or to be schooled, to be amazed or to be unleashed—whatever brings us to Philip's work—we are fortunate to have found it.

Evie Shockley
Jersey City, NJ
September 2014

Acknowledgments

The author would like to thank the Canada Council for its support, and the following journals for publishing some of the poems in this book: *(f.)Lip, Dandelion, Obsidian, Tiger Lily, Hambone,* and *Tessera.* "Testimony Stoops to Mother Tongue" is included in the anthology *Poetry by Canadian Women.*

In the poem sequence "And Over Every Land and Sea" quotations from *The Metamorphoses of Ovid,* translated with an introduction by Mary M. Innes (Penguin Classics, 1955), are reproduced with the kind permission of Penguin Books Ltd.; in the poem "She Tries Her Tongue" quotations from *Klein's Comprehensive Etymological Dictionary of the English Language* are reproduced with the kind permission of Elsevier Science Publishers B.V.; in "Universal Grammar" references are to Noam Chomsky's *Language and Responsibility* (Pantheon Books, 1977) and to *Grammatical Man* by Jeremy Campbell (Simon & Schuster, 1982); references to Cecily Berry's *Voice and the Actor* are reproduced by kind permission of Harrap General Books Ltd., first published by Harrap Ltd., 1973. Copyright Cecily Berry, 1973.

And Over Every Land and Sea

Meanwhile Proserpine's mother Ceres, with panic in her heart
vainly sought her daughter over all lands and over all the sea.

Questions! Questions!

Where she, where she, where she
be, where she gone?
Where high and low meet I search,
find can't, way down the islands' way
I gone—south:
day-time and night-time living with she,
down by the just-down-the-way sea
she friending fish and crab with alone,
in the bay-blue morning she does wake
with kiskeedee and crow-cock—
skin green like lime, hair indigo-blue,
eyes hot like sunshine-time;
grief gone mad with crazy—so them say.
Before the questions too late,
before I forget how they stay,
crazy or no crazy I must find she.

As for Cyane, she lamented the rape of the goddess . . .
nursing silently in her heart a wound that none could heal . . .

Adoption Bureau

Watch my talk-words stride,
like her smile the listening
breadth of my walk—on mine
her skin of lime casts a glow
of green, around my head indigo
of halo—tell me, do
I smell like her?
To the north comes the sometimes
blow of the North East trades—
skin   hair   heart   beat
and I recognize the salt
sea   the yet   else   and . . . something
again knows sweat   earth
the smell-like of I and she
the perhaps blood lost—

She whom they call mother, I seek.

3

It would take a long time to name the lands and seas over which the goddess wandered. She searched the whole world—in vain . . .

Clues

She gone—gone to where and don't know
looking for me looking for she;
is pinch somebody pinch and tell me,
up where north marry cold I could find she—
Stateside, England, Canada—somewhere about,
"she still looking for you—
try the Black Bottom—Bathurst above Bloor,
Oakwood and Eglinton—even the suburbs them,
but don't look for indigo hair and
skin of lime at Ontario Place,
or even the reggae shops;
stop looking for don't-see and can't—
you bind she up tight tight with hope,
she own and yours knot up in together;
although she tight with nowhere and gone
she going find you, if you keep looking."

When kindly day had dimmed the stars, still she sought
her daughter from the rising to the setting sun. She grew
weary with her efforts and thirsty too . . .

The Search

Up in the humpback whereabouts-is-that hills,
someone tell me she living—up
there in the up-alone cocoa hills of Woodlands,
Moriah, with the sky, and self, and the bad bad of grieving;
all day long she dreaming about wide black nights,
how lose stay, what find look like.
A four-day night of walk bring me
to where never see she:
is "come child, come," and "welcome" I looking—
the how in lost between She
and I, call and response in tongue and
word that buck up in strange;
all that leave is seven dream-skin:
sea-shell, sea-lace, feather-skin and rainbow-flower,
afterbirth, foreskin and blood-cloth—
seven dream-skin and crazy find me.

. . . the earth opened up a way for me and, after passing deep down through its lowest caverns, I lifted up my head again in these regions, and saw the stars which had grown strange to me.

Dream-skins

Dream-skins dream the dream dreaming:
(in two languages)

Sea-shell

>   low low over the hills
>   she flying
>   up up from the green of sea
>   she rise emerald
>   skin
>   fish belt
>   weed of sea crown she

Feather-skin

>   lizard-headed
>   i suckle her
>   suckling me
>   flat
>   thin like the
>   host
>   round and white
>   she swells enormous with
>   milk and child

Sea-lace

>   in one hand the sun
>   the moon in the other
>   round and round
>   she swing them from chains
>   let fly till they come
>   to the horizon
>   of rest

Rainbow-flower

six-limbed
my body dances
flight
from her giant promises
she reaches down
gently
snaps my head
a blooded hibiscus
from its body
crooning
she cradles the broken parts

Afterbirth

one breast
white
the other black
headless
in a womb-black night
a choosing—
one breast
neither black
nor white

Foreskin

a plant sprouts there—
from the mouth
mine
wise black and fat she laughs
reaching in for the tree
frees the butterfly
in-lodged
circles of iridescence
silence

Blood-cloth

<pre>
                    wide wide
                    i open my mouth
                              to call
                    the blood-rush come up
                                        finish
                    write she name
                    in the up-above sky
                    with some clean white rag
                    she band up my mouth
                         nice nice
</pre>

Blood-cloths
(dream in a different language)

<pre>
                  sand
                    silence
                        desert
                              sun
              the wide of open mouth
                    blood of rush
                    hieroglyphs
                    her red
                    inscriptions
                    her name
                    up-above sky
                                  sudden
                    clean of white
                                  cloths
                       wounded mouth
                    broad back
                                  hers
                    to tie
                       carry
                       bear

              "the voice, the voice, the voice"
                       she whispers
                       she walks
                       she whispers
                                  ceaselessly
</pre>

Ceres knew it (Proserpine's girdle) well, and as soon as she recognized it, tore her dishevelled hair, as if she had only then learned of her loss: again and again she beat her breast.

Sightings

Nose to ground—on all fours—I did once
smell that smell,
on a day of once—
upon a time, tropic with blue
when the new, newer and newest of leaves compete,
in the season of suspicion she passed,
then and ago trailed the wet and lost of smell;
was it a trompe l'oeil—
the voice of her sound, or didn't I once
see her song, hear her image call
me by name—my name—another sound, a song,
the name of me we knew she named
the sound of song sung long past time,
as I cracked from her shell—
the surf of surge
the song of birth.

For behold, the daughter I have sought so long has now at last been found—if you call it "finding" to be more certain that I have lost her, or if knowing where she is is finding her.

Adoption Bureau Revisited

blood-spoored
the trail follows
                    me
following her
                    north
                            as far as not-known
                            I trace it

                    dream-skins dream
                            the loss
                    ours and ancient
                        unfelled tears
                            harden
                    in the sun's attention
                            diamond
            the many-voiced one of one voice
                            ours
                    betrayal and birth-blood
                            unearthed

Something! Anything! of her.
She came, you say, from where
she went—to her loss:
"the need of your need"
in her groin

                        the oozing wound
                    would only be healed
                        on sacred ground
                        blood-spoored

                the trail . . .
                            following
                she
                        follows . . .

Cyclamen Girl

The Catechist

Early-blooming brown legs
satin-cotton
(was all the rage those days)
in their sheen and skinny;
around them
the confirmation dress crinolines stiff—
black girl white dress
—photograph circa 1960—
a stiff-petalled cyclamen
hot-housed
on green stalks of ignorance.
The finger now traces the negative
outline of the white dress
—or is it the positive form of the girl
where sudden edges meet?
Images blur—bleed into each other
as if the fixer didn't quite work,
or maybe it was the heat that caused the leak;
in those days nothing could be counted on—
least of all cyclamen girls
early bloomers in the heat of it all
with the lurking smell of early pregnancy.
So there, circa 1960, she stands—
black and white in frozen fluidity

                                   aging
photograph of the cyclamen girl
                                 caught between
blurred images of
                     massa and master.

Eucharistic Contradictions

with a speech spliced and spiced
into a variety of life and lies
sowbread host in we own ole mass of
double-imaged
doubly imagined
dubbed dumb
can't-get-the-focus-right reality
of mulatto   dougla   niggerancoolie
that escaped the so-called truth of the shutter—
confirms contradictions of church
                              god
                        doubt &
                        dogma
the cyclamen girl—yellowed confirmation dress—
(photograph circa 1960)
curls like copra left to dry
in the glare of unanswered questions
                                    away
from the brittle matrix of her coconut cocoon

The Catechism

A preparation more complex than learning about sin

                                      she

swung

      a skilled trapezist—
      no net
           below
      no one
           to catch

her

between

      the code of Victoria—
      no sex before marriage
      no love after

and

      the code of mama—
      "now you's a young lady
      you can press your hair"

Blood and deceit
twinned
in always

Vows

White
    satin ribbons
White
    cotton sox
White
    Bata shoes
White
    Book of Common Prayer
White
    satin-cotton confirmation dress
<u>White</u>
    <u>Soul</u>

The cyclamen girl
        stood
        ready
        to
Promise
    the triple lie
She
   who believed
   in and on
   <u>the "triune majesty"</u> —
            sunshine
          black skin &
            doubt
(in that order)

Transfiguration

In the ceremony of White
The cyclamen girl would answer
To her name

Aphrodite!

Gives rote answers
About promises
Of the godfathers

Ave Maria!

Remembering
First the drums
Then the women
Called out her name

Atabey!

Her other name

Oshun!

As she whirls
Into the circle of grief
For her fleeting childhood
Passed like the blood
Of her first menses
Quick and painful
Name her

Rhythm!
Song!
Drum!

Mahogany-tipped breast catches
The glare of the fires
Women of the moon feast and fast
And feast again

Name her

Aphrodite! Mary! Atabey! } water
Orehu! Yemoja! } goddesses
Oshun!

For her <u>newly arrived wound</u>
Name her!
empowerment?

The Communicant

His blood
        this
is my badge of fertility
            shed
red
    is my badge of futility
    month by red month
                 blood
          is the badge
            is the red

with moon-caked madness
                the waiting mouth
                    crushes
the body bro-
ken for all cyclamen girls

—or so they have been told

Epiphany

In a land of shadows
Herring-boned with memory,
The great stone-bird mother
Sweet-balmed with honey
Drops her daughters
From her open beak
—Like pebbles
Pebbles of blood and stone;
The cyclamen girl returns
To her own

cyclamen girl
—photograph circa 1960—

African Majesty

From Grassland and Forest
(The Barbara and Murray Frum Collection)*

*1981 Art Gallery of Ontario exhibit

African Majesty

From Grassland and Forest
(The Barbara and Murray Frum Collection)

Hot breath
        death-charred
winds
        depth-charged
words:
     rainfall
      magic
      power
the adorn of word
in meaning,
the mourn in loss
safe safety save
mute
muse
     museums
         of man—
Berlin, London, Paris, New York,
revenge seeks the word
in a culture mined
         to abstraction;
corbeaux circle
     circles of plexiglass
         death;
circles of eyes
circles for the eyes—

        wanderers
        in the centuries of curses
        the lost I's
        the lost equation:

            you plus I equals we
            I and I and I equals I
               minus you

alone or I
alone   circled
by the plexiglass of circles—
in a forest made-believe
                         filtered of fear
by light and the *au courant* of fashion
the wisdomed wood
stripped of reason
restored to 'living
proof' of primitive aesthetics:
"the African influence" on—
Braque, Picasso, Brancusi . . .
defies
        the blame in absolve
                  absolves

                  In the elsewhere of time
                  head   knees   eyes drop
                  earthward— they would have . . .
                  not now
                         feet pace
                  the circumference
                  plexiglass of circle that circles
                  prisons and prisms the real in once-upon-a-time-
                  there-was
                              mask   reliquary   fetish
                                             memory
                                             ancestor

to adorn the word with meaning
to mourn the meaning in loss

*Meditations on the Declension of Beauty
by the Girl with the Flying Cheek-bones.*

Meditations on the Declension of Beauty by the Girl with the Flying Cheek-bones

If not   If not   If

Not

If not in yours

              In whose

In whose language

Am I

If not in yours

              In whose

In whose language

Am I   I am

        If not in yours

In whose

        Am I

(if not in yours)

        I am yours

In whose language

            Am I not

Am I not   I am yours

If not in yours

If not in yours

            In whose

In whose language

        Am I . . .

Girl with the flying cheek-bones:
She is
I am
Woman with the behind that drives men mad
And if not in yours
Where is the woman with a nose broad
As her strength
If not in yours
In whose language
Is the man with the full-moon lips
Carrying the midnight of colour
Split by the stars — a smile
If not in yours

       In whose

In whose language

         Am I

         Am I not

         Am I   I am yours

         Am I not   I am yours

         Am I   I am

If not in yours
       In whose
In whose language
       Am I
If not in yours
       Beautiful

Discourse on the Logic of Language

Discourse on the Logic of Language

English
is my mother tongue.
A mother tongue is not
not a foreign lan lan lang
language
l/anguish
          anguish
—a foreign anguish.

English is
my father tongue.
A father tongue is
a foreign language,
therefore English is
a foreign language
not a mother tongue.

What is my mother
tongue
my mammy tongue
my mummy tongue
my momsy tongue
my modder tongue
my ma tongue?

I have no mother
tongue
no mother to tongue
no tongue to mother
to mother
tongue
me

I must therefore be
tongue
dumb
dumb-tongued
dub-tongued
damn dumb
tongue

EDICT 1
Fear

*Every owner of slaves
shall, wherever possible,
ensure that his slaves
belong to as many ethno-
linguistic groups as
possible. If they can-
not speak to each other,
they cannot then foment
rebellion and revolution.*

WHEN IT WAS BORN, THE MOTHER HELD HER NEWBORN CHILD CLOSE: SHE BEGAN THEN TO LICK IT ALL OVER. THE CHILD WHIMPERED A LITTLE, BUT AS THE MOTHER'S TONGUE MOVED FASTER AND STRONGER OVER ITS BODY, IT GREW SILENT—THE MOTHER TURNING IT THIS WAY AND THAT UNDER HER TONGUE UNTIL SHE HAD TONGUED IT CLEAN OF THE CREAMY WHITE SUBSTANCE COVERING ITS BODY.

Those parts of the brain chiefly responsible for speech are named after two learned nineteenth century doctors, the eponymous Doctors Wernicke and Broca respectively.

Dr. Broca believed the size of the brain determined intelligence; he devoted much of his time to 'proving' that white males of the Caucasian race had larger brains than, and were, therefore, superior to, women, Blacks and other peoples of colour.

Understanding and recognition of the spoken word takes place in Wernicke's area—the left temporal lobe, situated next to the auditory cortex; from there relevant information passes to Broca's area—situated in the left frontal cortex—which then forms the response and passes it on to the motor cortex. The motor cortex controls the muscles of speech.

but I have
a dumb tongue
tongue dumb
father tongue
and english is
my mother tongue
is
my father tongue
is a foreign lan lan lang
language
l/anguish
  anguish
a foreign anguish
is english—
another tongue
my mother
    mammy
    mummy
    moder
    mater
    macer
    moder
tongue
mothertongue

tongue mother
tongue me
mothertongue me
mother me
touch me
with the tongue of your
lan lan lang
language
l/anguish
  anguish
english
is a foreign anguish

EDICT II

Every slave caught speaking his native language shall be severely punished. Where necessary, removal of the tongue is recommended. The offending organ, when removed, should be hung on high in a central place, so that all may see and tremble.

THE MOTHER THEN PUT HER FINGERS INTO HER CHILD'S MOUTH—GENTLY FORCING IT OPEN; SHE TOUCHES HER TONGUE TO THE CHILD'S TONGUE, AND HOLDING THE TINY MOUTH OPEN, SHE BLOWS INTO IT—HARD. SHE WAS BLOWING WORDS—HER WORDS, HER MOTHER'S WORDS, THOSE OF HER MOTHER'S MOTHER, AND ALL THEIR MOTHERS BEFORE—INTO HER DAUGHTER'S MOUTH.

"it"
until now...
only becomes her daughter
after the mother's words
are in her mouth

32

A tapering, blunt-tipped, muscular, soft and fleshy organ describes
(a) the penis.
(b) the tongue.
(c) neither of the above.
(d) both of the above.

In man the tongue is
(a) the principal organ of taste.
(b) the principal organ of articulate speech.
(c) the principal organ of oppression and exploitation.
(d) all of the above.

The tongue
(a) is an interwoven bundle of striated muscle running in three planes.
(b) is fixed to the jawbone.
(c) has an outer covering of a mucous membrane covered with papillae.
(d) contains ten thousand taste buds, none of which is sensitive to the taste of foreign words.

Air is forced out of the lungs up the throat to the larynx where it causes the vocal cords to vibrate and create sound. The metamorphosis from sound to intelligible word requires
(a) the lip, tongue and jaw all working together.
(b) a mother tongue.
(c) the overseer's whip.
(d) all of the above or none.

Universal Grammar

Parsing—the exercise of telling the part of speech of each word in a sentence (Latin, pars, a part)

the—distinguishing adjective, limiting the noun, cell.

smallest—adjective of quantity, superlative degree, qualifying the noun, cell (unsuccessfully).

cell—common noun, neuter gender, singular number, third person, nominative case governing the intransitive verb, remembers. (Long-term memory improves cell growth in nerve cells.)

remembers—regular verb, transitive, active voice, indicative mood, present tense, singular number, third person agreeing with its nominative, cell which remembers and so re-members.

O—sound of exclamation as in O God! Made by rounding the lips;   first syllable of word name of African goddess of the river—O/shun.

Man
Man is
The tall man is
The tall, blond man is
The tall, blond, blue-eyed man is
The tall, blond, blue-eyed, white-skinned man is

MANY FACTORS AFFECT AND DETERMINE THE ORDER OF
WORDS IN A SPOKEN SENTENCE: THE STATE OF MIND OF
THE SPEAKER; THE GENDER OF THE SPEAKER; HIS OR HER
INTENTIONS; THE CONTEXT OF THE SPEECH; THE IMPRES-
SION THE SPEAKER WISHES TO MAKE; THE BALANCE OF
POWER BETWEEN SPEAKER AND LISTENER AND, NOT LEAST
OF ALL, THE CONSTRAINTS OF UNIVERSAL GRAMMAR

The tall, blond, blue-eyed, white-skinned man is shooting

the smallest cell
remembers
a sound
(sliding two semitones to return
home)
a secret order
among syllables
Leg/ba
O/shun
Shan/go

heart races
blood pounds
remembers
speech

fragments—*common noun, neuter gender, plural number, third person object of verb remembers. Re-membered fragments become whole.*

tremble—*regular verb, instransitive, used as a noun, lacking all attributes of the noun but movement. Only verbs have movement.*

ex—*prefix signifying in English and Latin 'out' or 'forth' as in exodus—the departure of the Israelites from the black land, Egypt; 'to remove', 'expel' or 'drive out' as in exorcize by use of a holy name like Legba, Oshun or Shango.*

man—*common noun, male gender, singular number, third person, nominative case governing the verb, is. And woman.*

again—*adverb used incorrectly as a noun modifying the transitive verb, forget, used incorrectly as a noun.*

fragments
                    brief
                as Sappho's
tremble of tongue on the brink of
ex/

> (when the passage of sound is completely
> blocked a consonant is called)

plosive
tongue on the brink of
ex/

> (prefix—occurring only before vowels)

odus
orcize
on the brink of
ex/

> (to strip or peel off (the skin) 1547)

coriate

The tall, blond, blue-eyed, white-skinned man is shooting

tongue trembles
on the again and again
of forget

THE THEORY OF UNIVERSAL GRAMMAR SUGGESTS THE WAY
WE LEARN LANGUAGE IS INNATE—THAT THE CONSCIOUS
MIND IS NOT AS RESPONSIBLE AS WE MIGHT BELIEVE IN
THIS PROCESS. OUR CHOICES OF GRAMMATICAL POSSIBIL-
ITIES AND EXPRESSIONS ARE, IN FACT, SEVERELY LIMITED;
IT IS THESE VERY LIMITATIONS THAT ENSURE WE LEARN
LANGUAGE EASILY AND NATURALLY.

Parsing—the exercise of dis-membering language into fragmentary cells that forget to re-member.

raped—regular, active, used transitively   the again and again   against women   participled into the passive voice as in, 'to get raped';   past present   future—tense(d) against the singular or plural number of the unnamed subject, man

when the smallest cell remembers—
how do you
how can you
when the smallest cell
                    remembers
lose a language

O homem alto, louro de olhos azuis esta a disparar
El blanco, rubio, alto de ojos azules está disparando
De lange, blanke, blonde man, met der blauwe ogen, is aan het schieten
Le grand homme blanc et blond aux yeux bleus tire sur
Der grosser weisse mann, blonde mit bleuen augen hat geschossen
The tall, blond, blue-eyed, white-skinned man is shooting

> *an elephant*
> *a native*
> *a wild animal*
> *a Black*
> *a woman*
> *a child*

somewhere

———————————————————————————————

Slip mouth over the syllable; moisten with tongue the word.
Suck   Slide   Play   Caress   Blow—Love it, but if the word
gags, does not nourish, bite it off—at its source—
Spit it out
Start again

From **Mother's Recipes on How to Make a Language Yours or
How Not to Get Raped.**

The Question of Language
is the Answer to Power

LESSONS FOR THE VOICE (1)

Vowels are by nature either long or short. In the following list the long ones appear in capital letters. These vowels are all shaped predominantly by the lips, though the position and freedom of the blade of the tongue affects their quality.

When practising these words, it is helpful to use a bone prop.

OO   *as in how did they 'lose' their word?*

oo   *as in 'look' at the spook.*

OH   *as in the slaves came by 'boat' (dipthongal).*

AW   *as in the slaves were valued for their 'brawn'.*

o   *as in what am I offered for this 'lot' of slaves?*

OW   *as in they faced the 'shroud' of their future (dipthongal).*

OI   *as in they paid for their slaves with 'coin' (dipthongal).*

word it off
speech it off
word in my word
word in your word
I going word my word
                    begin
the in of beginning   *OO as in how did they 'lose' a language.*
empires   *oo as in 'look' at the spook.*
            erect with new
"Make it new"
                    he said
"Make it new"
floundering in the old

                              but I fancy the new—
                                        in everything
                              insist upon it
                              the evidence of newness
                                                  is
                                        upon us
OH as in the slaves came   without nigger slave coolie
    by 'boat'.   the wog of taint
AW as in they were valued   the word
    for their 'brawn'.   that in the beginning was
                                        —not his
                              I decree it mine
                                        at centre
                              soft
                              plastic
                              pliable
                                  doing my bid as in
                                              smash
                              the in-the-beginning word
                                              centre
                              it at open
                                    clean-split

45

Facts to Remember

(1) Words collect emotional and physical responses.

(2) The larger the space, the more weight and friction is required on the consonant.

(3) Intention, sound and word together produce clarity.

(4) Anxiety to convey meaning often results in over emphasis and emphasis as a way of conveying meaning means that you are unconsciously holding on to meaning and limiting it.

(5) When you reach down for the sound, it is touched off like a drum; it releases itself and reaches as far as you wish. The sound is there to back the word.

to reveal the heart
                              pulse
that betrays as lover
                                        as
weapon

  jerk it
 dove it
 stew it
 cook it
      down
 run it down slow
 run it down tender
  till it come to do the bid in
we
    this chattel language
      babu english
      slave idiom
      nigger vernacular
      coolie pidgin
      wog pronunciation

*o as in what am I offered for this
  'lot' of slaves.*
*OW as in they faced the 'shroud' of
  their future.*
*OI as in they paid for their slaves
  with 'coin.'*

(I say old chap how goes it, what ho?)

this lingua franca
arrrrrrrrrgot of a blasted soul

(Helpful questions and commentary)

(1) *Within the holds of the slave ship, how much weight and friction would be necessary to convey the meaning of life?*

(2) *Intention, sound and word of death would come together with astonishing clarity to banish anxiety—anxiety to convey the meaning of life.*

(3) *By holding on to the meaning of life, did the slaves unconsciously limit it—or merely the word?*

(4) *How far down would they have to reach for a sound that would banish the future, restore the past and back their word in the present?*

(5) *Do words collect historical responses?*

"The word, the word"

                              the Red Queen screamed

"Banish the word
Off with its head—
The word is dead
The word is risen
Long live the word!"

"Oh dear, oh dear," said Alice, "what will Tigger and Pooh and Eeyore and Mrs. Tiggy Winkle think of all this kerfuffle. She does carry on so—that Red Queen."

*Testimony Stoops to Mother Tongue**

*Robert Browning, *The Ring and the Book*

Testimony Stoops to Mother Tongue

> 'Tis a figure, a symbol, say;
> A thing's sign: now for the thing signified.
> Robert Browning, *The Ring and the Book*

I

Stone mourns

        haunted

into shape and form

by its loss

      upon

        loss

honed keen

as the feel of some days

at the very centre of every word,

the as-if of yesterday it happened;

mind and body concentrate

           history—

the confusion of centuries that passes

as the word

      kinks hair

      flattens noses

      thickens lips

      designs prognathous jaws

      shrinks the brain

to unleash the promise

        in ugly

the absent in image.

II
those who would

                inhabit

the beyond of pale

where the sacrilege of zero

                    disputes

the mathematic of heart,

erect shrines of stone to the common

                          in us

       —anathema—

touch tongue to tongue

                  release

the strange sandwiched between

tongue and cheek and lip

III

the somewhere of another mother's tongue

                      tongues

                        licks

into nothing

the prison of these walled tongues

—speaks

        this/

        fuck-mother motherfuckin-

        this/

        holy-white-father-in-heaven-

        this/

        ai! ai!

            tongue

that wraps

  squeezes

the mind round

          and around

IV

this tongue that roots

                           deep

in

   yank

   pull

   tear

   root

out

that I would

              chop

                   in

pieces

        a snake

each to grow

           a head

Medusa

(Gorgon—

to turn my tongue to stone)

           a tail

and haunt the absence

         that mourns

/haunted into shape and form. . . . .

V

Oh, but shall I?

                I shall

tame them—

            these snakes

feed them

        milk

from black breasts

                    (stroke and caress into
lactate)
                         to hush
the slithered silk of tongues
                                        split
—sliver and silver into forty pieces—
words ride again
                         across
mared nights

let me—
          I shall
lie
    with them
    bed them with silence
these snakes
                         wisdomed
with the evil
                         of words
to breed the again and
again
                         in breed
—a new breed
—a race
—a warrior race
                         of words
—a nest-egg
                         that waits
to hatch the ever
                         in wait

VI
shall I
     strike
under tongue and foot
them
     —these words
hold in aloft
         up
in either hand
         harmless
the word
     that claims
and maims
     and claims
again
or
     in my mother's mouth
     shall I
         use
the father's tongue
cohabit in strange
mother
     incestuous words
     to revenge the self
         broken
upon
     the word

She Tries Her Tongue; Her Silence Softly Breaks

She Tries Her Tongue; Her Silence Softly Breaks

All Things are alter'd, nothing is destroyed
Ovid, *The Metamorphoses* (tr. Dryden).

the me and mine of parents
the we and us of brother and sister
the tribe of belongings small and separate,
when gone . . .
on these exact places of exacted grief
i placed mint-fresh grief coins
sealed the eyes with certain and final;
in such an equation of loss tears became
a quantity of minus.
with the fate of a slingshot stone
loosed from the catapult pronged double with history
and time on a trajectory of hurl and fling
to a state active with without and unknown
i came upon a future biblical with anticipation

It is important, when transplanting plants, that their roots not be exposed to the air longer than is necessary. Failure to observe this caution will result in the plant dying eventually, if not immediately. When transplanting, you may notice a gently ripping sound as the roots are torn away from the soil. This is to be expected: for the plant, transplanting is always a painful process.

The Practical Guide to Gardening

seek   search and   uproot
the forget and remember of root words
uncharged
            pathways electric with the exposed lie
circuits of dead
            currents of still
                        words
synapses of unuse and gone
                        words
wordless
            in the eden of first sin
                        and
naked

1. *The limbic system along with the hypothalamus, hippocampus, amygdala, fornix and olfactory bulb rule the basic drives for food, sex and survival.*
2. *The limbic system or primitive cortex plays a significant role in emotions; it is indispensable in the formation of memory.*
3. *Human memory may be either immediate, short-term, or long-term.*
4. *The cerebral cortex is the storehouse of our memory—it makes us human.*
5. *What we choose to store in our long-term memory is closely linked to our emotions.*
6. *Memory is essential to human survival.*

Facts to Live By and Die

without the begin of word
grist in a grind and pound of together
in the absence of a past mortared with

                                apart

the harsh husk of a future-present begins

. . . and the big bad wolf came and said,
  "Little pig, little pig let me in."
  "No, no, not by the hair of my chinny chin chin."
  "Then I'll huff and I'll puff and I'll blow your
  house in."
  The wolf huffed and puffed and he huffed and puffed
and couldn't blow the house down.

  The first pig built his house of straw; the second of wood. Did the third pig buy his bricks or was he given them, and why? Where did he get his money to buy his bricks with?
  Straw, wood or brick. The moral of this tale, is that the right choice of materials secures safety.

How to Build Your House Safe and Right

oath   moan   mutter   chant
            time grieves the dimension of other
babble   curse   chortle   sing
            turns on its axis of silence
praise-song   poem   ululation   utterance
            one song would bridge the finite in silence
syllable   vocable   vowel   consonant
            one word erect the infinite in memory

. . . the day of Pentecost was fully come . . .

And suddenly there came a sound from heaven as of a rushing mighty wind, and it filled all the house where they were sitting.

And there appeared unto them cloven tongues like as of fire, and it sat upon each of them.

And they were filled with the Holy Ghost, and began to speak with other tongues . . .

. . . every man heard them speak in his own language.

The Acts of the Apostles *2: 1,2,3,4,6.*

absencelosstears   laughter   grief
in any language
                    the same
only larger
            for the silence
                            monstrosity
obscenity
tongueless wonder
blackened stump of a tongue
                            torn
out
            withered
            petrified
                            burnt
on the pyres of silence
a mother's child foreign
                            made
by a tongue that cursed
                        the absence
in loss
tears   laughtergrief
                    in the word

. . . and if a stranger were to touch her newborn child, the mother will have nothing to do with it. She can smell the stink of the stranger on her child and will refuse to suckle it, believing the spirit of her child to be taken by the stranger.

De Matribus et Advenis*

*On Mothers and Strangers

I do not presume to come to this thy table
father forgive
most merciful father, trusting in my own righteousness
foreign father forgive
but in thy manifold and great mercies.
forgive her   me   this foreignness
I am not worthy so much as to gather up the crumbs under thy table
forgive me this dumbness
but thou art the same Lord, whose property
this lack of tongue forgive
is always to have mercy
                                        upon

                                                                this
                                        thisthisand this
                                                    disfigurement this
                                                                            dis
                                        memberment
                                                    this
                                                                verbal crippling
                                                                            this
                                        absence of voice
                                                            that
                                        wouldnotcould   not
        sing

Kyrie eleison
Christos eleison
Kyrie eleison

Is it in the nature of God to forgive himself—
For his sin?

The Book of unCommon Prayer

Hold we to the centre of remembrance
that forgets the never that severs
word from source
and never forgets the witness
of broken utterances that passed
before   and now
breaks the culture of silence
in the ordeal of testimony;
in the history of circles
each point lies
along the circumference
diameter or radius
each word creates a centre
circumscribed by memory . . . and history
waits   at rest always

still at the centre

*history, n—L. historia, 'narrative, story, narration, account', from Gk . . .
'learning by inquiry, knowledge obtained by inquiry; account of one's inqui-
ries; narration, historical narrative; history . . .*

*memory, n—ME. memoire, fr OF. memorie (F. Memoire), fr. L. memoria,
'memory', fr. memor, 'mindful', which stands for *me-mor, and derives
from I.-E. *mer-(s)mer-, reduplication of base *(s)mer-, to care for, be
anxious about, think, consider, remember' . . .*
Cp. memoir, commemorate, remember. Cp. also martyr, mourn, smriti.

**Klein's Comprehensive Etymological
Dictionary of the English Language**

Without memory can there be history?

That body should speak
When silence is,
Limbs dance
The grief sealed in memory;
That body might become tongue
Tempered to speech
And where the latter falters
Paper with its words
The crack of silence;
That skin become
Slur   slide   susurration
Polyphony and rhythm—the drum;
The emptied skull a gourd
                                        filled
With the potions of determine
That compel the split in bridge
Between speech and magic
Force and word;
The harp of accompaniment the ribcage
Strung with the taut in gut;
Flute or drumstick the bones.
When silence is
Abdication of word   tongue and lip
Ashes of once in what was
. . . Silence
Song   word   speech
Might I . . . like Philomela . . . sing
                                        continue
                                                over
                                                    into

. . . pure utterance

. . . and on the day of the great salmon run, the first salmon caught is cooked and shared among the elders—men and women. The oldest woman of the tribe, accompanied by the youngest girl-child, then goes down to the waters and returns the skeleton whole to its watery home. This is the way the tribe ensures future gifts of winter food.

Of Women, Wisdom, Fishes and Men

Afterword

The Absence of Writing or How I Almost Became a Spy

I wasn't hard-backed but I definitely wasn't no spring chicken when I started to write—as a way of living my life I mean, although like a lot of women I had been doing it on the quiet quiet filling up all kinds of notebooks with poems, thinkings—deep and not so deep—curses and blessings.

The last thing I expected to end up doing was writing, and when I upsed and left a safe and decent profession—second oldest in the world, they say—for writing, I was the most surprised person. Is in those growing up years as a child in Trinidad and Tobago that you will find the how, why and wherefore of this take-me-by-surprise change.

If someone had asked me when I was growing up to tell them what pictures came to mind when I heard the word 'writer' I would have said nothing. What I wanted to be most of all was a spy, and after reading about spies in World War II, spying was much more real to me than writing. After all there was an Empire and we, its loyal subjects, had to defend it. Black and brown middle class people—my family, short on money but long on respectability, belonged to this class—wanted their children to get 'good jobs' and, better yet, go into the professions. Massa day was done and dreams were running high high—my son, the doctor! Education was open to everyone, girl and boy alike—my daughter, the lawyer! And if your son or daughter didn't manage to get that far, there was always nursing, teaching or accounting. Failing that there was always the civil service.

Some people might say that this was normal since the writers we had heard about—all white—had usually starved and you couldn't say this about doctors or lawyers. Education was going to be the salvation of the black middle classes—so we believed—and a profession was the best proof that you had put servitude behind you, and were becoming more like the upper classes. Writing was no help in this at all.

In high school I was learning and learning about many things—English literature, French history, American history and finally in my fifth year, West Indian history—poor-ass cousin to English history and the name V.S. Naipaul was there somewhere. V.S. Naipaul, writer. It was a sister of his who taught me in high school who first mentioned him to us, her students. But V.S. Naipaul was Indian and, in the context of Trinidad at that time, in the eyes of the blacks, this was a strike against him. V.S. Naipaul, the writer, we didn't understand or care to understand. Maybe, without knowing it, we were already understanding how he was going to use us in his writing life.

Books for so! I wasn't no stranger to them—they were all around since my father was a headmaster and living in the city meant I could get to the library easily. Books for so! Rows and rows of them at the library as greedy-belly I read my way through Dostoevsky, Moravia, Shakespeare, Dickens. Books for so! Other people were writing them. I was reading them.

I wasn't different from any of the twenty or so girls in my sixth-form class. None of them were looking to writing as a career, or even thinking the thought as a possibility. Profession, vocation, career—we all knew those words; we, the black and brown middle classes, scholarship girls whom our teachers were exhorting to be the cream of society, the white salt of the earth. Profession, vocation, career—anything but writer.

Some people are born writing, some achieve writing and some have writing thrust upon them. My belonging is to the last group, coming slowly to accept the blessing and yoke that is writing, and with so doing I have come upon an understanding of language—good-english-bad-english english, Queenglish and Kinglish—the anguish that is english in colonial societies. The remembering—the revolutionary language of 'massa day done'—change fomenting not in the language of rulers but in the language of the people.

Only when we understand language and its role in a colonial society can we understand the role of writing and the writer in such a society; only then, perhaps, can we understand why writing was not and still, to a large degree, is not recognized as a career, profession, or way of be-ing in the Caribbean and even among Caribbean people resident in Canada.

What follows is my attempt to analyse and understand the role of language and the word from the perspective of a writer resident in a society which is still very much colonial—Canada; a writer whose recent history is colonial and which continues to cast very long shadows.

Fundamental to any art form is the image, whether it be the physical image as created by the dancer and choreographer, the musical image of the composer and musician, the visual image of the plastic artist or the verbal image, often metaphorical, of the writer and poet. (For the purposes of this essay I will be confining myself for the most part to the concept of image as it relates to the writer.) While, however, it may be quite easy to see the role of image as it relates to the visual artist, it may be less easy to do so with respect to the writer. The word 'image' is being used here to convey what can only be described as the irreducible essence—the i-mage—of creative writing; it can be likened to the DNA molecules at the heart of all life. The process of giving tangible form to this i-mage may be called i-maging, or the i-magination. Use of unconventional orthography, 'i-mage' in this instance, does not only represent the increasingly conventional deconstruction of certain words, but draws on the Rastafarian practice of privileging the 'I' in many words.[1] 'I-mage' rather than 'image' is, in fact, a closer approximation of the concept under discussion in this essay. In her attempt to translate the i-mage into meaning and non-meaning, the writer has access to a variety of verbal techniques and methods—comparison, simile, metaphor, metonymy, symbol, rhyme, allegory, fable, myth—all of which aid her in this process. Whatever the name given to the technique or form, the function remains the same—that of enabling the artist to translate the i-mage into meaningful language for her audience.

The power and threat of the artist, poet or writer lies in this ability to create new i-mages, i-mages that speak to the essential being of the people among whom and for whom the artist creates. If allowed free expression, these i-mages succeed in altering the way a society perceives itself and, eventually, its collective consciousness. For this process to happen, however, a society needs the autonomous i-mage-maker for whom the i-mage and the language of any art form become what they should be—a well-balanced equation.

When, in the early 1900s, Picasso and his fellow artists entered their so-called 'primitive stage' they employed what had traditionally been an African aesthetic of art and sculpture and succeeded in permanently altering the sensibilities of the West toward this aesthetic. In the wake of European colonial penetration of Africa and Oceania the entire art world was, in fact, revolutionized and the modernist art movement was born. These changes did not necessarily increase the understanding or tolerance of the West for Africans and Africa, but people began to perceive differently.

I-mages that comprised the African aesthetic had previously been thought to be primitive, naive, and ugly, and consequently had been dismissed not only by white Westerners, but by the Africans themselves living outside of Africa—so far were Africans themselves removed from their power to create, control and even understand their own i-mages. The societies in which these New World Africans lived—North and South America, England, the Caribbean—lacked that needed matrix in which the autonomous i-mage-maker could flourish. The only exception to this is to be found in musical traditions, where despite the hostility of these predominantly white societies, the African i-mage-maker in musical art forms was successful in producing authentic art which has also permanently influenced Western music.

Caribbean society has been a colonial society for a much longer time than not, and the role of the i-mage, i-mage-making, and i-mage control are significant. The societies that comprise the Caribbean identity may be identified by:

(a) a significant lack of autonomy in the creation and dissemination of i-mages;

(b) opposition by the ruling classes both at home and abroad to the creation of i-mages that challenge their i-mage making powers and the status quo;

(c) restricting of indigenously created i-mages to marginal groups, e.g. reggae and calypso.

While changes like independence have improved some of these circumstances both within the Caribbean and within Caribbean societies in the large metropolitan centres overseas, these factors continue to affect the artist and particularly the writer. The tradition of writing for the Caribbean and Caribbean people is a brief one, and briefer still is the Afro-centric tradition in that writing.

I argued above that at the heart of all creative writing is the i-mage; the tangible presentation of this is the word, or word symbol as I prefer to describe it. The success of the execution of this i-mage, be it poetical or in the extended metaphor of the novel, depends to a large degree on the essential tension between the i-mage and word or words giving voice to the i-mage. Tension is created by the interplay of i-mage and word—i-mage creating word, word giving rise to further i-mage and so on. This process is founded upon familiarity with word and i-mage, 'familiarity' being used here in the sense of being kin to, a part of, related to. What is assumed here, but probably should not be, is also a growing familiarity with be-ing and how it relates to the outer world.

If this process is as it should be, then the autonomous i-mage-maker serves the function of continually enriching the language by enlarging the source of i-mages—in particular, metaphorical i-mage. If we accept that living language continually encapsulates, reflects and refines the entire experiential life and world view of the tribe, the race and consequently of society at large; and if we accept that the poet, the story-teller, the singer or balladeer (through their words), express this process in their work, then we must accept that this process becomes one way in which a society continually accepts, integrates and transcends its experiences, positive or negative. For it is through those activities—poetry, story-telling and writing—that the tribe's experiences are converted and transformed to i-mage and to word almost simultaneously, and from word back to i-mage again. So metaphorical life takes place, so the language becomes richer, the store of metaphor, myth and fable enlarged, and the experience transcended not by exclusion and alienation, but by inclusion in the linguistic psyche, the racial and generic memory of the group.

The progenitors of Caribbean society as it exists today created a situation such that the equation between i-mage and word was destroyed for the African. The African could still think and i-mage, she could still conceive of what was happening to her. But in stripping her of her language, in denying the voice power to make and, simultaneously, to express the i-mage—in denying the voice expression, in fact—the ability and power to use the voice was effectively stymied. We could go further and argue that with the withering of the word in the New World, not only did the i-mage die, but also the capacity to create in one's own i-mage. The bridge that language creates, the crossover from i-mage to expression was destroyed, if only temporarily. Furthermore, alien and negative European languages would replace those African languages recently removed and, irony of all ironies, when the word/i-mage equation was attempted again, this process would take place through a language that was not only experientially foreign, but also etymologically hostile and expressive of the non-being of the African. To speak another language is to enter another consciousness. Africans in the New World were compelled to enter another consciousness, that of their masters, while simultaneously being excluded from their own. While similar prohibitions extended to music at various times, language was one of the most important sites of struggle between the Old World and the New World. The outcome of this struggle was the almost absolute destruction and obliteration of African languages. Together with the accompanying act of renaming by the European, this was one of the most devastating and successful acts of aggression carried out by one people against another. African musical art forms probably owe their survival and persistence to the fact that they were essentially non-verbal.

Once the i-mage making power of the African had been removed or damaged by denial of language and speech, the African was then forced back upon the raw experience without the linguistic resources to integrate and eventually transcend it. The resulting situation became one in which the African was decontextualised, except in so far as her actions generated profits for the owners. The language within which that decontextualisation flourished was in itself and *at best* a decontextualised one for the African. At worst the language would serve to destroy. Language, therefore, succeeded in pushing the African further away from the expression of her experience and, consequently, the meaning of it.

The African in the Caribbean could move away from the experience of slavery in time; she could even acquire some perspective upon it, but the experience, having never been reclaimed and integrated metaphorically through the language and so within the psyche, could never be transcended. To reclaim and integrate the experience required autonomous i-mage makers and therefore a language with the emotional, linguistic, and historical resources capable of giving voice to the particular i-mages arising out of the experience. In summing up his efforts to augment the English language in the sixteenth century, Sir Thomas Elyot wrote, "I intended to augment our Englyshe tonge, whereby men should as well expresse more abundantly the thynge that they conceyved in theyr harts (wherefore language was ordeyned) hauynge wordes apte for the pourpose." That the African needed to express "more abundantly the thynge . . . they conceyved in theyr harts" is undisputed; that the English language lacked "wordes apte for the pourpose" cannot be denied. Over and above her primary function as a chattel and unit of production, the English language merely served to articulate the non-being of the African. The purpose for which language was ordained would remain unfulfilled. 1 would argue further that it is impossible for any language that inherently denies the essential humanity of any group or people to be truly capable of giving voice to the i-mages of experiences of that group without tremendous and fundamental changes within the language itself. In the instant case, however, since there was no possible expression of the New World experience within any African language, the i-maging could only be expressed through the English language.

Essentially, therefore, what the African would do is use a foreign language expressive of an alien experiential life—a language comprised of word symbols that even then had affirmed negative i-mages about her, and one which was but a reflection of the experience of the European ethnocentric world view. This would, eventually, become her only language, her only tool to create and express i-mages about herself, and her life experiences, past, present and future. The paradox at the heart of the acquisition of this language is that the African learned both to speak and to be dumb at the same time, to give voice to the experience and i-mage, yet remain silent. That silence has had profound effect upon the English-speaking African Caribbean artist working in the medium of words.

Speech, voice, language, and word—all are ways of being in the world, and the artist working with the i-mage and giving voice to it is being in the world. The only way the African artist could be in this world, that is the New World, was to give voice to this split i-mage of voiced silence. Ways to transcend that contradiction had to and still have to be developed, for that silence continues to shroud the experience, the i-mage and so the word. As the poet, Cecilia Bustamente, writes in *The Poet and Her Text*:

> . . . within this radius (of language) she discovers that having adapted herself as a vehicle of communication for historical and cultural moments between a dominant culture and a dominated one, language is

becoming one more tool of subordination, replacement, pressure and distortion. Its potential is unexpressed, a proof that it suffers from margination of the dominated, or rather—the threat of being unable to internalize her own culture which has been violated. In order to express this reality, the social function of language fosters either its communicative values or **silence** [my emphasis]. Reflecting a similar stress it detects the multiple structures of violence, its authenticity is tested in the confusion of recognition in the tense structures of violation and domination that, whether paradoxical or contrary, are always obstructive. . . . This is the dilemma of the dominated: to disappear or change at the prices of their lives.

Concerning literature and the Caribbean, C.L.R. James has written that "language for us is not a distillation of our past."[2] If by 'language' is meant Queen's or King's English as we know it, this statement is true, because that language, for all the reasons given above, can never be a distillation of our past. But what the ordinary African, the African on the Papine bus, or the Port-of-Spain route taxi, or the Toronto subway, produced from the only linguistic behaviour allowed her—that is, functionality (at its barest level) in the English language—is truly and surely a distillation of her past. It may not be the clearest distillation, but it remains a distillation all the same.

In the vortex of New World slavery, the African forged new and different words, developed strategies to impress her experience on the language. The formal standard language was subverted, turned upside down, inside out, and even sometimes erased. Nouns became strangers to verbs and vice versa; tonal accentuation took the place of several words at a time; rhythms held sway. Many of these 'techniques' are rooted in African languages; their collective impact on the English language would result in the latter being, at times, unrecognizable as English. Bad English. Broken English. Patois. Dialect. These words are for the most part negative descriptions of the linguistic result of the African attempting to leave her impress on the language. That language now bears the living linguistic legacy of a people trying and succeeding in giving voice to their experience in the best and sometimes the only way possible. The havoc that the African wreaked upon the English language is, in fact, the metaphorical equivalent of the havoc that coming to the

New World represented for the African. Language then becomes more than a distillation, it is the truest representation, the mirror i-mage of the experience.

Language of the people. Language for the people. Language by the people, honed and fashioned through a particular history of empire and savagery. A language also nurtured and cherished on the streets of Port-of-Spain, San Fernando, Boissiere Village and Sangre Grande in the look she dey and leh we go, in the mouths of the calypsonians, Jean and Dinah, Rosita and Clementina, Mama look a boo boo, the cuss buds, the limers, the hos (whores), the jackabats, and the market women. These are the custodians and lovers of this strange wonderful you tink it easy jive ass kickass massa day done Chagaramus is we own ole mass pretty mass pansweet language. A more accurate description of this language would be to call it a demotic variant of English. The Caribbean demotic. The excitement for me as a writer comes in the confrontation between the formal and the demotic within the text itself.

In the absence of any other language by which the past may be repossessed, reclaimed and its most painful aspects transcended, English in its broadest spectrum must be made to do the job. To say that the experience can only be expressed in standard English (if there is any such thing) or only in the Caribbean demotic (there *is* such a thing) is, in fact, to limit the experience for the African artist working in the Caribbean demotic. It is *in the continuum of expression* from standard to Caribbean English that the veracity of the experience lies.

One can never be less than self-conscious as an African Caribbean writer working in any of the demotic variants of English, whether the demotic variant be a form of standard English or Caribbean English. And for the writer from the Caribbean, language must always present a dilemma. At its most simple, the dilemma can be resolved to an either/or dichotomy: either one writes in a demotic variant of English, or one writes in straight English. Choice of one or the other in this scenario is often seen as a political choice and much bad writing takes place on either side of the divide in the name of linguistic validity. It is not sufficient, however, to write only in dialect, for too often that remains a parallel and closed experience, although a part of the same language. Neither is it sufficient to write only in what we have come to call standard English. The language as we know it has to be dislocated and acted upon—even destroyed—so that it begins to serve our purposes. It is our only language, and while it is our mother tongue, ours is also a father tongue. Some writers—Derek Walcott and Wilson Harris immediately come to mind—have publicly acknowledged their gratitude for the 'blessing' conferred on them by the imposition of the English language and have, in fact, refused to acknowledge that there even exists a dilemma; others like Earl Lovelace have taken up the challenge that the anguish that is English presents for all African Caribbean people.

The issue is, however, more complex than the either/or dichotomy suggests. The place African Caribbean writers occupy is one that is unique, and one that forces the writer to operate in a language that was used to brutalize and diminish Africans so that they would come to a profound belief in their own lack of humanity. No language can accomplish this—and to a large degree English did—without itself being profoundly affected, without itself being tainted. The challenge, therefore, facing the African Caribbean writer who is at all sensitive to language and to the issues that language generates, is to use the language in such a way that the historical realities are not erased or obliterated, so that English is revealed as the tainted tongue it truly is. Only in so doing will English be redeemed.

Subversion of the language has already taken place. It began when the African in the New World through alchemical (al kimiya, the art of the black and Egypt) practices succeeded in transforming the leavings and detritus of a language and infused it with her own remembered linguistic traditions. Much more must now be attempted. If we accept the earlier premises, that at the heart of the language lies the i-mage, metaphorical or otherwise, and that to the artist falls the task of articulating and presenting this image to the people, then the attack must be made at the only place where any true change is ever possible: at the heart of the language—the i-mage and the simultaneous naming of it. The African artist in the Caribbean and in the New World must create in, give voice to and control her own i-mages. This is essential for any group, person, or people, but more so for the African in the New World, since in one sense, our coming upon ourselves, our revelation to ourselves in the New World was simultaneous with a negative re-presentation of ourselves to ourselves, by a hostile imperialistic power, and articulated in a language endemically and etymologically hostile to our very existence. In a very real sense, it can be argued that for the African in the New World learning the English language was simultaneous with learning of her non-being, her lack of wholeness.

The experience of the African in the Caribbean and the New World is now, however, as much part of the English collective experience as England is part, for better or worse, of the African experience (in the same manner, for instance, that Germany will always be a part of the Jewish collective experience and vice versa). That experience expressed in the language—a language that is shared yet experientially different for both groups—has been and continues to be denied, hence terms like broken or bad English, or good English, all of which serve to alienate the speaker even further from her experience. If the language is to continue to do what language must do; if it is to name and give voice to the i-mage and the experience behind that i-mage—the thing we conceive in our hearts—and so house the being, then the experience must be incorporated in the language and the language must begin to serve the re-creation of those i-mages.

There are certain historical and sociological, not to mention etymological, reasons why when we hear certain words and phrases, such as 'thick lips' or 'kinky hair', the accompanying images are predominantly negative; such expressions connote far more than they denote. From whose perspective are the lips of the African thick or her hair kinky? Certainly not from the African's perspective. How then does the writer describe the Caribbean descendants of West Africans so as not to connote the negativity implied in descriptions such as 'thick lips'?

Journal entry Dec. 11, 1986 (Testimony stoops to Mother Tongue)
I want to write about kinky hair and flat noses—maybe I should be writing about the language that kinked *the hair and* flattened *noses, made* jaws prognathous . . .

This was how I tried to meet this particular challenge in a particular poem; it is but a small example of the challenge facing the African Caribbean writer who is interested in making English her home. The challenge is to re-create the images behind these words so that the words are being used newly.

The African in the Caribbean and the New World is as much entitled to call the English language her own, as the Englishman in his castle.

However, just as we have had to make that i-mage our own, so too must he be made to acquire our i-mages, since we are both heirs to a common language, albeit to different linguistic experiences. Our experiences have touched, in both negative and positive ways, and we remain forever sensitive to each other through the language.

For too long, however, we have been verbal or linguistic squatters, possessing adversely what is truly ours. If possession is, in fact, nine-tenths of the law, then the one-tenth that remains is the legitimisation process. It is probably the hardest part, this reclaiming of our image-making power in what has been for a long time a foreign language. It must be done.

It is, perhaps, ironic that New World Africans, descendants of cultures and societies where the word and the act of naming was the focal point and fulcrum of societal forces,[3] should find themselves in a situation where the word, their word and the power to name was denied them. Traditionally, for instance, in many West African societies, until named, a child did not even acquire a recognizable and discernible human identity. In the New World after the destruction of the native peoples, Africans would be renamed with the name of the stranger. If what the artist does is create in her own i-mage and *give name* to that i-mage, then what the African artist from the Caribbean and the New World must do is create in, while giving name to, her own i-mage—and in so doing eventually heal the word wounded by the dislocation and imbalance of the word/i-mage equation. This can only be done by consciously restructuring, reshaping and, if necessary, destroying the language. When that equation is balanced and unity of word and i-mage is once again present, then and only then will we have made the language our own.

This is not a conclusion

What happens when you are excluded from the fullness and wholeness of language?
What happens when only one aspect of a language is allowed you—as woman?
—as Black?
What happens when the language of ideas is completely removed and nothing is given to replace it?

Surely thought requires language—how can you, without language, think or conceptualize?

87

What happens to a language that is withheld or only used in a particular way with its users—does it become dissociated?
—one level business
—one level orders, commands, abuses, brutality
—one level education to a specific purpose and level

What of celebration?
What of love?
What of trust between individuals?

There can be no conclusion to the issues raised in this essay since language is always and continually changing—a fluid phenomenon. One version of this paper was published many years ago in the journal *Fireweed* (1983), and at that time I called this section Postscript and wrote that it was "not a conclusion because the issues raised here are still very much undecided." The questions I raised then were "how does one begin to destroy a language? How does one replace the image behind the word?" I replied then that those questions remained unanswered and would "probably remain so for a long time." I am now struck at how prescient I was in that original article about many of the issues I was to deal with in my writing subsequent to the writing of the paper. The Absence of Writing could be seen as something of a blueprint for my poetic and writing life.

Have I answered those questions, or do they still remain unanswered? I believe I have come closer to answering them than I did six years ago. The manuscript, *She Tries Her Tongue*, has taken me a long way towards the goal of decentring the language. This is not the same thing as destroying a language which is a far harder thing to do. Also, destruction connotes great sturm und drang when, in fact, what works just as well at times is a more subtle but equally profound approach. For instance in the poem, 'Discourse on the Logic of Language', the issue that I raised in the earlier Postscript—that of father tongue vis-à-vis a mother tongue, some sort of balance is achieved despite the anguish of English, and despite the fact that English is both a mother tongue and a father tongue. In the accompanying journal I kept as I worked on *She Tries Her Tongue* I write as follows:

I am laying claim to two heritages—one very accessible, the other hidden. The apparent accessibility of European culture is dangerous and mislead-

ing especially what has been allowed to surface and become de rigueur. To
get anything of value out of it, one has to mine very, very deeply and only
after that does one begin to see the connections and linkages with other
cultures. The other wisdoms—African wisdom needs hunches, gut feelings
and a lot of flying by the seat of the pants, free falls only to be caught at the
last minute. It calls for a lot more hunting out of the facts before one can
even get to the essence, because in almost exact reversal with European
culture not much has been allowed to surface—am almost tempted to say
that one can, for that reason, trust that information more.

I must add now that lack of information bears directly on one's ability
to make i-mages.

The linguistic rape and subsequent forced marriage between African
and English tongues has resulted in a language capable of great rhythms
and musicality; one that is and is not English, and one which is among
the most vital in the English-speaking world today. The continuing chal-
lenge for me as a writer/poet is to find some deeper patterning—a deep
structure, as Chomsky puts it—of my language, the Caribbean demotic.
The challenge is to find the literary form of the demotic language. As
James Baldwin has written, "Negro speech is not a question of drop-
ping s's or n's or g's but a question of the beat."[4] At present the greatest
strength of the Caribbean demotic lies in its oratorical energies which
do not necessarily translate to the page easily. Just as the language that
English people write is not necessarily or often that which is spoken by
them, so, too, what is spoken in the streets of Trinidad, or by some Carib-
bean people in Toronto, is not always going to be the best way of express-
ing it on the page. To keep the deep structure, the movement, the kinetic
energy, the tone and pitch, the slides and glissandos of the demotic
within a tradition that is primarily page-bound—that is the challenge.

In the former Postscript, I wrote that it was "perhaps, ironic that a
critique of the use and role of English in a particularly brutal, historical
context should be written in standard English, but that in itself throws
into sharp relief the dilemma described above." I was not completely sat-
isfied with my argument then that the dilemma as to what language was
appropriate was answered by my argument that the English language in
its complete range belonged to us, and whatever mode best suited our
needs should be used. In fact, the problem was that the piece itself did

not, as I now believe it ought to, reflect that range that I spoke of. Unlike the former piece, the opening paragraphs of the present piece, explaining the absence of writing in my early life, are written closer to the Caribbean demotic than to standard English. Could or ought I to have continued the entire piece in this style? Perhaps, but I do believe that the present piece is a far truer reflection of how I function linguistically than the original one.

While I continue to write in my father tongue, I continue the quest I identified in 1983 to discover my mother tongue, trying to engender by some alchemical practice a metamorphosis within the language from father tongue to mother tongue. Will I recognize this tongue when I find it, or is it rather a matter of developing it rather than finding it? Whatever metaphorical i-mages one uses—discovery or development—the issue of recognition is an important one, since implied within the word itself is the meaning, the i-mage of knowing again.

There was a profound eruption of the body into the text of *She Tries Her Tongue*. This represents a significant development for me as a poet. The manuscript has become a blaze along a poetic path. In the New World, the female African body became the site of exploitation and profoundly anti-human demands—forced reproduction along with subsequent forceful abduction and sale of children. Furthermore, while the possibility of rape remains the amorphous threat it is, the female body continues to be severely circumscribed in its interaction with the physical surrounding space and place. How then does this affect the making of poetry, the making of words, the making of i-mages if poetry, as I happen to believe, "begins in the body and ends in the body"?[5] *She Tries Her Tongue* is the first blaze along the path to understanding and resolving this particular conundrum.

I continue, as I did in the former Postscript, to see the issue as being one of power, and so control. I still, as I did then, fear being reductionist, but writing does entail control in many areas—control of the word, control of the i-mage, control of information which helps in the process of i-mage-making and, equally important, control in the production of the final product. By the time the manuscript *She Tries Her Tongue* comes into print it will be almost two years and many, many rejections after its completion, despite its winning the *Casa de las Americas* prize in 1988. As a female and a black living in a colonial society of Trinidad and Tobago, control was absent in each of these areas, hence the absence of writing, especially creative writing, and hence the lack of recognition of writing as a possible vocation or profession. As a female and a black presently living in a society that is, in many respects, still colonial (I refer here to Canada's relationship with the United States of America), and a society which is politely but vehemently racist, while I may have gained some control of my word and its i-mage-making capacities, control of information and production is still problematic.

For the many like me, black and female, it is imperative that our writing begin to recreate our histories and our myths, as well as integrate that most painful of experiences—loss of our history and our word. The reacquisition of power to create in one's own i-mage and to create one's own i-mage is vital to this process; it reaffirms for us that which we have always known, even in those most darkest of times which are still with us, when everything conspired to prove otherwise—that we belong most certainly to the race of humans.

ENDNOTES

1   Readers interested in exploring Rastafarian language further are referred to the works of the Jamaican writer, Valma Pollard.

2   C.L.R. James, "The Artist in the Caribbean," in *The Future in the Present* (Westport: Lawrence & Co., 1977), p. 184.

3   Janheinz Jahn, *Muntu* (New York: Grove Press Inc., 1961), p. 125.

4   Conversations with James Baldwin, ed., Fred L. Standley & Louis H. Pratt, (University Press of Mississippi, 1989).

5   Burnshaw, Stanley, *The Seamless Web* (New York: George Braziller Inc., 1970).

ABOUT THE AUTHOR

M. NourbeSe Philip is a poet, essayist, novelist and playwright who was born in Tobago and now lives in Toronto. She practiced law in Toronto for seven years before deciding to write fulltime. Philip has published four books of poetry, one novel, and three collections of essays. She was awarded a Pushcart Prize (1981), the Casa de las Americas Prize (Cuba, 1988), the Tradewinds Collective Prize (1988), and was made a Guggenheim Fellow in Poetry (1990). Her most recent book of poetry is *Zong!* (Wesleyan, 2008), a moving work of experimental verse.

Evie Shockley was born and raised in Nashville, Tennessee, and received her BA from Northwestern University. After getting her J.D. from University of Michigan Law School, she earned her MA and PhD in English from Duke University. Her books of poetry include *the new black* (Wesleyan, 2011), winner of the Black Caucus of ALA's Literary Award for Poetry, and *a half-red sea* (Carolina Wren Press, 2006), in addition to two chapbooks. She also has a book of criticism, *Renegade Poetics: Black Aesthetics and Formal Innovation in African American Poetry* (Iowa, 2011). Shockley's honors include the Holmes National Poetry Prize and fellowships from Cave Canem, the Millay Colony for the Arts, the American Council of Learned Societies, and the Schomburg Center for Research in Black Culture of the New York Public Library.